Three Chord
Acoustic Songs

ISBN 978-1-4803-6653-4

HAL•LEONARD®
CORPORATION
7777 W. BLUEMOUND RD. P.O. BOX 13819 MILWAUKEE, WI 53213

Visit Hal Leonard Online at
www.halleonard.com

	D
Verse 2	I wish I was like you, easily amused.

Find my nest of salt, ev'rything is my fault.

I'll take all the blame, aqua seafoam shame.

Sunburn, freezer burn, choking on the ashes of her enemy.

	G
Chorus 2	In the sun, in the sun I feel as one.

In the sun, in the sun.

A
Married, married.

Married, buried, yeah, yeah, yeah, yeah.

Interlude 　|**D**　　　|　　　　|　　　　|　　　　|

	D
Outro	‖: All alone is all we all are.

All alone is all we all are. :‖　***Play 5 times***

All alone is all we all,

All alone is all we all are.

All alone is all we all are.

Big Yellow Taxi

Words and Music by
Joni Mitchell

Open D tuning:
(low to high) D-A-D-F♯-A-D

(Capo 2nd fret)

G   A   D

Intro

| G | | A | | |
| D | | | | |

Verse 1

        G   D
They paved paradise, put up a parking lot

               G   D   A   D
With a pink ___ hotel,   a boutique, and a swinging hot spot.

Chorus 1

D
Don't it always seem to go

That you don't know what you've got 'till it's gone?

       G   D   A   D
They paved paradise,   put up a parking lot.

                             (‖: Shoo, bop, bop, bop, bop. :‖)

Verse 2

           G   D
They took all the trees, put 'em in a tree mu - seum.

              G   D   A   D
And they charged the people   a dollar and a half just ___ to see 'em.

Chorus 2   *Repeat Chorus 1*

Verse 3

   G   D
Hey, farmer, farmer, put away that D.D.T., now.

       G   D
Give me spots on my apples,

     A   D
But leave me the birds and the bees. Please!

Chorus 3   *Repeat Chorus 1*

Verse 4

   G   D
Late last night I heard the screen door slam,

      G   D   A   D
And a big yellow taxi ___ took a - way my old man.

Chorus 4

   D
Don't it always seem to go

That you don't know what you've got 'till it's gone?

     G   D A   D
They paved paradise,   put up a parking lot.
                              (Shoo, bop, bop, bop, bop.)

Outro-Chorus

            D
I said, don't it always seem to go

That you don't know what you've got 'till it's gone?

     G   D A   D
They paved paradise,   put up a parking lot.
                              (Shoo, bop, bop, bop, bop.)

     G   D A   D
They paved paradise,   put up a parking lot.
                              (Shoo, bop, bop, bop, bop.)

     G   D A   D
They paved paradise,   put up a parking lot. *Ha, ha, ha.*

Blowin' in the Wind

Words and Music by
Bob Dylan

Melody:

How man-y roads

(Capo 7th fret)

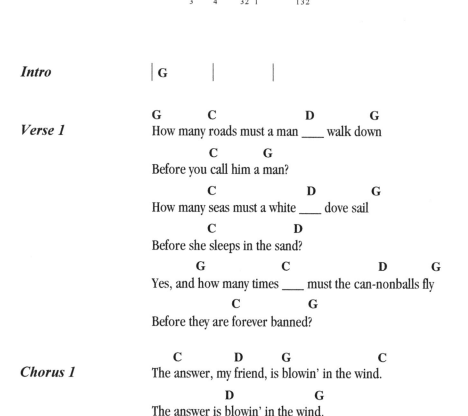

Intro
| G | | |

Verse 1

G   C   D   G
How many roads must a man ___ walk down
           C   G
Before you call him a man?
           C   D   G
How many seas must a white ___ dove sail
           C   D
Before she sleeps in the sand?
      G   C   D   G
Yes, and how many times ___ must the can-nonballs fly
             C   G
Before they are forever banned?

Chorus 1

        C   D   G   C
The answer, my friend, is blowin' in the wind.
           D   G
The answer is blowin' in the wind.

| Interlude 1 | | C | | D | | G | | C | |
| | | | | D | | G | | | | |

Verse 2

                    G   C   D   G
Yes, and how many years__ can a moun - tain exist

                   C   G
Before it is washed to the sea?

                           C   D   G
Yes, and how many years can some people exist

                      C   D
Before they're al-lowed to be free?

               G   C   D   G
Yes, and how many times ____ can a man ____ turn his head

                        C   G
And pretend that he just ____ doesn't see?

Chorus 2   *Repeat Chorus 1*

Interlude 2   *Repeat Interlude 1*

Verse 3

                    G   C   D   G
Yes, and how many   times must a man look up

                     C   G
Before he can see ____ the sky?

                         C   D   G
Yes, and how many ears ____ must one man have

                      C   D
Before he can hear __ people cry?

              G   C   D   G
Yes, and how many deaths will it take till he knows

                    C   G
That too many peo - ple have died?

Chorus 3   *Repeat Chorus 1*

Outro   *Repeat Interlude 1*

Bye Bye Love

Words and Music by Felice Bryant
and Boudleaux Bryant

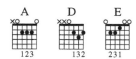

Intro |A | | D |A |

Chorus 1

D   A
Bye bye, love.

D   A
Bye bye, happiness.

D   A
  Hello loneliness.

       E   A
I think I'm gonna cry.

D   A
Bye bye, love.

D   A
Bye bye, sweet caress.

D   A
  Hello emptiness.

      E   A
I feel like I could die.

      E   A
Bye bye, my love, good-bye.

Verse 1

N.C.   E
There goes my baby

A
With someone new.

E
She sure looks happy,

A
I sure am blue.

D
She was my baby

E
Till he stepped in.

Goodbye to romance

A
That might have been.

Chorus 2   *Repeat Chorus 1*

Verse 2

E
I'm through with romance,

A
I'm through with love.

E
I'm through with counting

A
The stars a-bove.

D
And here's the reason

E
That I'm so free,

My loving baby

A
Is through with me.

Chorus 3

> **D**   **A**
> Bye bye, love.
>
> **D**   **A**
> Bye bye, happiness.
>
> **D**   **A**
>   Hello loneliness.
>
>   **E**   **A**
> I think I'm gonna cry.
>
> **D**   **A**
> Bye bye, love.
>
> **D**   **A**
> Bye bye, sweet caress.
>
> **D**   **A**
>   Hello emptiness.
>
>   **E**   **A**
> I feel like I could die.

>   **E**   **A**
> ‖: Bye bye, __ my love, good-bye. :‖   ***Repeat and fade***

Can't You See

Words and Music by
Toy Caldwell

Melody:

Gon-na take a freight train   down at the

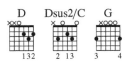

D   Dsus2/C   G

Intro ‖: D | Dsus2/C | G | D :‖ *Play 5 times*

Verse 1
D   Dsus2/C
Gonna take a freight train,   down at the station, Lord,

G   D
   I don't care where it goes.

                        Dsus2/C
Gonna climb a mountain,   the highest mountain.

G   D
   I jump off, nobody gonna know.

Chorus 1
                   D   Dsus2/C
Can't you see, ____ whoa, can't you see

           G   D
What that woman, Lord, she been doin' to me?

                    Dsus2/C
Can't you see, can't you see

           G   D
What that woman, she been doin' to me?

Verse 2	**D** **Dsus2/C** I'm gonna find me a hole in the wall,	

G   **D**
I'm gonna crawl inside and die.

        Dsus2/C
Come later now, a mean old woman, Lord,

G   **D**
Never told me goodbye.

Chorus 2   *Repeat Chorus 1*

Guitar Solo 1 ‖: **D** |**Dsus2/C** |**G** |**D** :‖

Verse 3
D   **Dsus2/C**
I'm gonna buy a ticket now, as far as I can

G   **D**
Ain't never comin' back.

        Dsus2/C
Grab me a southbound all the way to Georgia now,

G   **D**
Till the train, it run out of track

Chorus 3   *Repeat Chorus 1*

Guitar Solo 2 *Repeat Guitar Solo 1*

Chorus 4

D   Dsus2/C
Can't you see, whoa, ____ can't you see

     G   D
What that woman, Lord, she been doin' to me?

                           Dsus2/C
Can't you see, whoa, can't you see

     G   D
What that woman, she been doin' to me?

                        Dsus2/C
(Can't you see.) Oh, she's such a cra - zy lady.

                 G   D
(What that woman.)What that woman, she been doin' to me?

                          Dsus2/C
(Can't you see) Lord, I can't stand it no ____ more.

                 G   D
(What that woman.) Oh, she's been doin' to me.

Verse 4

               D
(Can't you see) ____ I'm gonna take a freight train

               D/C
(Can't you see) ____ Down at the station, Lord

               G   D
(What that woman) Ain't never comin' back. ____ Oh, no.

(Can't you see) Gonna ride me a southbound, now,

               D/C
(Can't you see) ____ All the way to Georgia, Lord

               G   D
(What that woman) Till the train, it run out a track.

Guitar Solo 3   *Repeat Guitar Solo 1*

Outro | D | Dsus2/C | G | D   ‖

Closer to Free

Words and Music by Sam Llanas
and Kurt Neumann

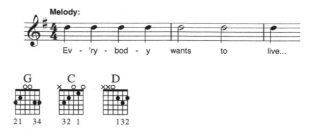

Intro |G |C |D |C |

Verse 1

      G   C   D
Ev'rybody wants to live

            C
Like they want to live,

        G   C   D
And ev'rybody wants to love

            C
Like they want to love.

G   C   D C   G
Ev'rybody wants to be closer to__ free.

Verse 2

      G   C   D
Ev'rybody wants re-spect,

          C
Just a little bit.

G   C   D
And ev'rybody needs a chance

              C
Once in a while.

G   C   D C   G   C D C
Ev'rybody wants to be closer to__ free.

Bridge 1

    C   D
Ev'rybody one,

    C   D
Ev'rybody two,

    C   D
Ev'rybody free.

Verse 3

    G   C   D
Ev'rybody needs to touch,

          C
You know, now and then.

      G   C   D
And ev'rybody wants a good,

      C
Good friend.

G   C   D C   G   C D C
Ev'rybody wants to be closer to___ free.

Verse 4   **Repeat Verse 2**

Bridge 2   ***Repeat Bridge 1***

               G   **C**   **D**
Verse 5   Ev'rybody wants to live

                      C
Like they want to live,

                 G   **C**   **D**
And ev'rybody wants to love

                    C
Like they want to love.

G   **C**   **D C**   **G**   **C** **D**
Ev'rybody wants to be closer to__ free.

        C   **G**   **C D**
Yeah, closer to__ free,

        C   **G**   **C D**
Yeah, closer to free,

C   **G**   **C D** **C**
Closer to__ free.

Outro   ‖: G |C |D |C   :‖   ***Play 4 times***
           ‖: G |C |D |C   :‖   ***Play 4 times***
           | G |

Daughter

Words and Music by Stone Gossard,
Jeffrey Ament, Eddie Vedder,
Michael McCready and
David Abbruzzese

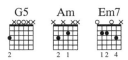

Intro | G5 | | |
          | | Am | |

Verse 1

G5
A - lone, listless,

        Am
Breakfast table in an otherwise empty room.

G5
Young girl, violins,

        Am
Center of her own attention.

G5
Mother reads aloud, child tries to understand it,

        Am
Tries to make her proud.

Pre-Chorus 1

G5   Em7
The shades go down. It's in her head,

Painted room, can't deny

There's something wrong.

Chorus 1

G5
   Don't call me daughter, not fit to.

          Am
The picture kept will remind me.

G5
   Don't call me daughter, not fit to.

          Am
The picture kept will remind me.

G5
   Don't call me...

Interlude 1

| Em7 | | | |
| | G5 | | |

Bridge

Em7
   She holds the hand that holds her down.

          She will rise above.

Guitar Solo

‖: G5 | | |
| | :‖

Chorus 2

G5
    Don't call me daughter, not fit to.

The picture kept will remind me.

Don't call me daughter, not fit to be.

        Am
The picture kept will remind me.

G5
    Don't call me daughter, not fit to.

        Am
The picture kept will remind me.

G5
    Don't call me daughter, not fit to be.

        Am   **G5**
The picture kept will remind me. Don't call me...

Interlude 2   ‖: Em7 | :‖ *Play 4 times*

Outro

Em7
    The shades go down.

The shades go down.

The shades go, go, go.

Drive

Words and Music by Brandon Boyd,
Michael Einziger, Alex Katunich,
Jose Pasillas II and Chris Kilmore

Melody:

Some-times   I   feel _ the fear _ of ____

Em   Cmaj7   A7

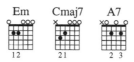

Intro   ‖: Em | Cmaj7   A7 :‖ *Play 4 times*

Verse 1
    Em   **Cmaj7**   **A7**
    Sometimes I feel the fear of

    Em   **Cmaj7** **A7**
Un-certainty stinging clear.

  Em   **Cmaj7**
  And I, I can't help but ask myself

A7   **Em**   **Cmaj7** **A7**
How much I'll let the fear take the wheel and steer.

Pre-Chorus 1
  Cmaj7   **A7**
  It's driven me be-fore,

                 Cmaj7
And it seems to have a vague,

A7   **Cmaj7**
Haunting mass appeal.

       A7
But lately I'm beginning to find that

 Cmaj7   **A7**
I ____ should be the one behind the wheel.

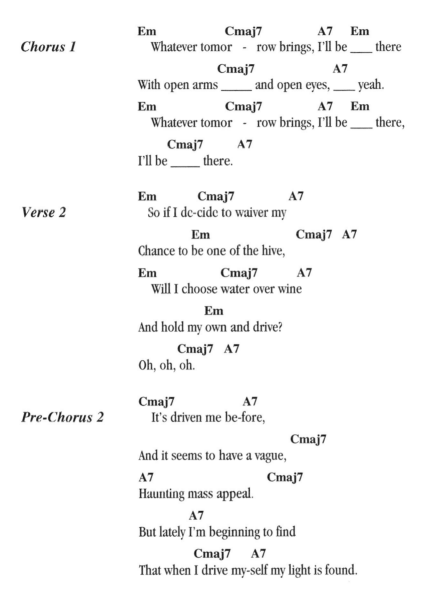

Chorus 1

```
Em              Cmaj7           A7    Em
   Whatever tomor  -  row brings, I'll be ___ there
                Cmaj7                A7
With open arms _____ and open eyes, ___ yeah.
Em              Cmaj7           A7    Em
   Whatever tomor  -  row brings, I'll be ___ there,
       Cmaj7        A7
I'll be _____ there.
```

Verse 2

```
Em        Cmaj7           A7
   So if I de-cide to waiver my
            Em                  Cmaj7  A7
Chance to be one of the hive,
Em            Cmaj7        A7
   Will I choose water over wine
             Em
And hold my own and drive?
         Cmaj7   A7
Oh, oh, oh.
```

Pre-Chorus 2

```
Cmaj7             A7
   It's driven me be-fore,
                          Cmaj7
And it seems to have a vague,
A7                    Cmaj7
Haunting mass appeal.
         A7
But lately I'm beginning to find
         Cmaj7     A7
That when I drive my-self my light is found.
```

Chorus 2	*Repeat Chorus 1*
Interlude	*Repeat Intro*

Cmaj7   **A7**   **Cmaj7**

Pre-Chorus 3   Would you choose a, water over wine?

A7   **N.C.**

Hold the wheel and drive.

Chorus 3   *Repeat Chorus 1*

Em   **Cmaj7**   **A7**

Outro   Do, do, do, ___ do, do, do,

          Em

Do, do, do, ___ do.

        Cmaj7

No, no, _____ no.

    A7   **Em**

Do, do, do, do, do.

          Cmaj7   **A7**

Do, do, do, do, ___ do, do, do,

          Em

Do, do, do, ___ do.

        Cmaj7   **A7** **Cmaj7** **A7**

No, no, _____ no, no, no.

For What It's Worth

Words and Music by
Stephen Stills

Melody:

There's some-thin' hap-pen-in' here, ___

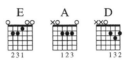

E	A	D

231   123   132

Intro |E   A | E | A | E |

Verse 1

E   A
    There's somethin' happenin' here,

   E   A
What it   is ain't exactly clear.

   E   A
There's a man with a gun over there,

      E   A
A, tellin' ____ me I got to be - ware.

Chorus 1

           E   D
I think it's time we stop. Children, what's that sound?

A
Ev'rybody look what's goin' down.

Interlude 1   *Repeat Intro*

Verse 2

```
E                            A
    There's battle lines be - ing drawn,
            E                   A
A, nobod - y's right if ev'rybod-y's wrong.
E                              A
    Young people speakin' their minds,
            E                      A
A, gettin' ___ so much resistance    from behind.
```

Chorus 2

```
                E        D
            It's time we stop. Hey, what's that sound?
A
Ev'rybody look what's goin' down.
```

Interlude 2   *Repeat Intro*

Verse 3

```
E                   A
    What a field day for ___ the heat,
E                   A
A thousand people in the street
            E                 A
Singin' ___ songs and a, carryin' signs.
            E                 A
Most - ly say, "Hooray, for our side."
```

Chorus 3   *Repeat Chorus 2*

Interlude 3 | E   A | E | A | |

Verse 4

       E   **A**
Paranoia strikes ___ deep,

       E   **A**
   Into your life it will ___ creep.

       E   **A**
It starts when you're always a - fraid.

             E   **A**
Step out ___ of line, the man come and ___ take you away.

Chorus 4

            E   **D**
We better stop. Hey, what's that sound?

A
Ev'rybody look what's goin'.

            E   **D**
We better stop. Hey, what's that sound?

A
Ev'rybody look what's goin'.

            E   **D**
We better stop. Now, what's that sound?

A
Ev'rybody look what's goin'.

            E   **D**
We better stop. Children, what's that sound?

A
Ev'rybody look what's goin'.

Outro |**E**   **D** |**A** |**E**   **D** | ‖ *Fade out*

The First Cut Is the Deepest

Words and Music by
Cat Stevens

I would have giv-en you all ___ of my heart, ___

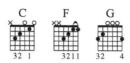

Intro ‖: C F G | |C F G | :‖

Verse 1
>   C   G   F G
> I would have given you all ___ of my heart,
>
>   C   G   F G
> But there's someone who's torn it apart.
>
>   C   G   F
> And she's taken just all ___ that I had.
>
>   G   C   G   F
> But, if you want, I'll   try to love again. ___ Oh, babe
>
> G   C   F   G
> Baby, I'll try ___ to love a - gain, but I know.

Chorus 1
>   C   G   F
>   The first cut is the deep - est.
>
> G   C   G   F   G
> Baby, I know   the first cut is the deep - est.
>
>   C   G   F   G
> Cause when it comes to bein' lucky she's cursed.
>
>   C   F   G
> When it comes to lovin' me, she's worse.

Verse 2	C G F G I still want you by ___ my side.

        C   G   F G
Just to help me dry the tears that I cried.

         C   G   F
And I'm sure gonna give you a try.

     G   C   G   F
And, if you want, I'll try to love again.

G   C   F   G
Baby, I'll try __ to love a - gain, but I know.

Chorus 2	*Repeat Chorus 1*
Guitar Solo	*Repeat Verse 1 (Instrumental)*
Verse 3	*Repeat Verse 2*
Chorus 3	*Repeat Chorus 1*
Intro	|C F G| |C F G| ||

Free Fallin'

Words and Music by
Tom Petty and Jeff Lynne

Melody:

She's a good girl, — loves her ma - ma,

(Capo 1st fret)

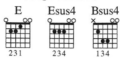

E	Esus4	Bsus4
2 3 1	2 3 4	1 3 4

Intro | E Esus4 | E Bsus4 | E Esus4 | E Bsus4 |

Verse 1
      E Esus4   E   Bsus4
She's a good girl, loves ___ her mama,

      E Esus4   E   Bsus4
Loves Je - sus, and Amer - ica too.

      E Esus4 E   Bsus4
She's a good girl, cra-zy 'bout Elvis,

      E   Esus4   E   Bsus4 E Esus4 E Bsus4
Loves hor - ses and her boy - friend, too.

Verse 2
      E Esus4   E   Bsus4
And it's a long day livin' in Re - seda.

      E Esus4   E   Bsus4
There's a free - way runnin' through the yard.

      E Esus4   E Bsus4
And I'm a bad boy 'cause I don't even miss her.

      E Esus4   E   Bsus4
I'm a bad boy for break - in' her heart.

Chorus 1
      E Esus4 E Bsus4 E   Esus4 E Bsus4
Now I'm free,   free fallin'.

      E Esus4 E Bsus4 E   Esus4 E Bsus4
Yeah, I'm free,   free fallin'.

Verse 3

         E   Esus4   E   Bsus4
Now all the vam - pires walkin' through the valley

      E   Esus4   E   Bsus4
Move west down Ventu - ra Boule - vard.

        E   Esus4   E   Bsus4
And all the bad boys are standin' in the shadows.

       E   Esus4   E   Bsus4
And the good girls are home with broken hearts.

Chorus 2   *Repeat Chorus 1*

Interlude 1 |E   Esus4 | E Bsus4 |

E   Esus4   E Bsus4
(Free fallin', I'm a free fallin', I'm a…)

|E   Esus4 | E Bsus4 |

E   Esus4   E Bsus4
(Free fallin', I'm a free fallin', I'm)

Verse 4

       E   Esus4 E   Bsus4
I wanna glide down o - ver Mul - holland,

       E   Esus4 E   Bsus4
I wanna write her name in the sky.

        E Esus4 E Bsus4
I'm gonna free fall out into nothin',

       E   Esus4   E   Bsus4
Gonna leave this world for a while.

Chorus 3   *Repeat Chorus 1*

Interlude 2 *Repeat Interlude 1*

Outro

        E Esus4 E Bsus4 E   Esus4 E Bsus4
Yeah, I'm free,   free fallin'.   Oh!

   E   Esus4   E Bsus4
||: (Free fallin', I'm a free fallin', I'm a) :|| *Repeat and fade*

Hold My Hand

Words and Music by
Darius Carlos Rucker,
Everett Dean Felber,
Mark William Bryan and
James George Sonefeld

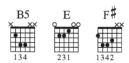

Intro

‖: B5   E | B5   E   :‖

Verse 1

      B5 E   B5   E
With a little love   and some tenderness,

     B5   E   B5   E
We'll walk upon the water, we'll rise above the mess.

      B5   E   B5   E
With a little   peace   and some harmony,

   B5   E   B5   E
We'll take the world to - gether, we'll take 'em by the hand.

Pre-Chorus 1

F#   E   B5
 'Cause I got a hand ___ for you.

F#   E   B5
 'Cause I wanna run with you.

Verse 2

      B5 E   B5   E
Yesterday ___   I saw you standing there.

   B5   E
Your head was down, your eyes were red,

   B5   E
No comb had touched your hair.

      B5 E   B5   E
I said, "Get up, ___   and let me see ___ you smile.

   B5   E   B5   E
We'll take a walk to - gether,   walk the road a while."

Pre-Chorus 2
      F♯   E   B5
'Cause ___ ('Cause I got a hand for you.) I got a hand for you.

      F♯   E   B5
('Cause I wanna run with you.) Won't you let me run with you, yeah.

Chorus 1
      B5   E F♯
(Hold my hand.) Want you to hold my hand.

      B5   E F♯
(Hold my hand.) I'll take you to a place where

      B5   E F♯
(Hold   my hand.)
You can be   anything you wanna be because

      E
I wanna love you the best that, the best that I can.

Interlude   *Repeat Intro*

Verse 3
                 B5   E   B5   E
You see, I was wast - ed   and I was wasting time.

      B5   E   B5   E
Till I thought about your problems, I thought about your crime.

          B5   E   B5   E
Then I stood up, ___   and then I screamed ___ aloud,

      B5   E
"I don't wanna be part of your problems,

      B5   E
Don't wanna be ___ part of your crowd, no."

Pre-Chorus 3
      F♯   E   B5
'Cause I got a hand for you. I got a hand for you.

      F♯   E   B5
'Cause I wanna run with you. Won't you let me run with you.

Chorus 2

B5   E   F#
(Hold my hand.) I want you to hold my hand.

B5   E   F#
(Hold my hand.) I'll take you to the promised land.

B5   E   F#
(Hold my hand.) Maybe we can change the world.

     E
But   I wanna love you the best that, the best that I can.

Guitar Solo

| B5   E | B5   E | B5   E | B5   E |
| F# E B5 | | F# E B5 | |

Chorus 3

B5   E   F#
(Hold my hand.) Want you to hold my hand.

B5   E   F#
(Hold my hand.) I'll take you to a place where

B5   E F#
(Hold   my hand.)
You can be   anything you wanna be because

E
  I, oh, no, no, no, no, no.

Chorus 4

B5   E   F#
(Hold my hand.) I want you to hold my hand.

B5   E   F#
(Hold my hand.) I'll take you to the promised land.

B5   E   F#
(Hold my hand.) Maybe we can change the world.

     E   B5 E
But   I wanna love you the best that, the best that I can.

   B5 E   B5 E B5 E
Oh, ___   the best that I can.

If I Were a Carpenter

Words and Music by
Tim Hardin

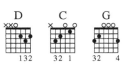

D   C   G

Intro | D | C | D | C |

Verse 1

       D   C   G   D
If I were a carpenter,   and you were a lady,
               C   G   D
Would you marry me anyway,   would you have my baby?
       C   G   D
If a tinker were my trade,   would you still love me,
       C   G   D
Carrying the pots I made,   following be - hind me?

Chorus 1

C   D
Save my love through loneliness,
G   D
Save my love for sorrow.
            C
I've given you my onliness,
G   D
Come and give me your to - morrow.

Verse 2

D   C   G   D
If I worked my hands in wood,   would you still love me?
          C   G   D
Answer me, babe, "Yes I would,   I'd put you a - bove me."
       C   G   D
If I were a miller,   at a mill wheel grinding,
          C   G   D
Would you miss your colored box,   your soft shoes shining?

Chorus 2   *Repeat Chorus 1*

The Joker

Words and Music by Steve Miller,
Eddie Curtis and Ahmet Ertegun

Some peo-ple call me __ the Space Cow - boy. __

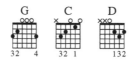

Verse 1

    G   C   D   C
Some people call me the Space Cowboy.

        G   C   D C
Yeah ___ some call me the Gangster of Love.

    G   C   D   C
Some people call me Maur - ice,

        G   C   D C
'Cause I speak of the pompatus of love.

G C   D   C
    People talk about ___ me, baby.

G   C   D   C
    Say I'm do - ing wrong, do - ing you wrong.

G   C   D   C
    Well, don't you worry, ba - by, don't wor - ry,

        G   C   D   C
'Cause I'm right here, right here, right here, right here at home.

Chorus 1

                G   C
'Cause I am a picker, I'm a grinner,

        G   C
I'm a lover, and I'm a sinner.

G   C   D   C
   I play my mu - sic in the sun.

        G   C
I'm a joker, I'm a smoker,

        G   C
I'm a midnight tok - er.

G   C   D
   I get my lov - ing on the run.

Oo, hoo. Oo, hoo.

Guitar Solo 1   ‖: G   C |D   C   :‖ ***Play 4 times***

             G   C   D   C
Verse 2   You're the cutest thing ___ that I ev - er did see.

      G   C   D   C
I really love your peach - es, want to shake your tree.

G   C   D   C
   Lovey dove - y, lovey dovey, lovey dovey all the time.

G   C   D   C
   Oo, wee, ba - by, I'll sure show you a good time.

Chorus 2   'Cause I am a picker, I'm a grinner,

       G   C
I'm a lover, and I'm a sinner.

G   C   D C
    I play my mu - sic in the sun.

       G   C
I'm a joker, I'm a smoker,

       G   C
I'm a midnight tok - er.

G   C   D C
    I sure don't want ___ to hurt no one.

Guitar Solo 2 | G   C | G   C | G   C | D   C |
                   | G   C | G   C | G   C | D | |
                                            Oo, hoo. Oo, hoo.

       G   C   D   C
Outro-Verse   Peo - ple keep talking about ___ me, baby.

G C   D C
    Say I'm doing you wrong.

G   C   D   C
    Well, don't you worry, don't worry, no don't wor - ry mama

G   C   D C
    'Cause I'm right here at home.

G C   D   C
    You're the cutest thing I ever did see.

    G   C   D   C
I really love your peaches, want to shake your tree.

G   C   D   C
    Lovey dove - y, lovey dovey, love - y dovey all the time.

G   C   D   C
    Come on, babe, ___ and I'll show you a good time.   ***Fade out***

Leaving on a Jet Plane

Words and Music by
John Denver

Melody:

All   my   bags   are packed,

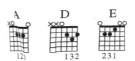

Intro

| A | D | | |
| A | E | | |

Verse 1

         A   D
All my bags are packed, I'm ready to go,

       A   D
I'm standing here out - side your door,

       A   F#m   E
I hate to wake you up to say good - bye.

                  A   D
But the dawn ___ is breaking, it's early morn',

      A   D
The taxi's waiting, he's blowing his horn,

      A   E
Al - ready I'm so lonesome I could ___ cry.

Chorus 1

> A   D
> So kiss me and smile for me,
>
> A   D
> Tell me that you'll wait for me,
>
> A   E
> Hold me like you'll never let me go.
>
>   A   D
> I'm leaving on a jet plane,
>
> A   D
>   I don't know when I'll be back again.
>
> A   D E
>   Oh, babe, I hate to go.

Verse 2

>   A   D
> There's so many times I've let you down,
>
>   A   D
> So many times I've played around,
>
> A   E
> I tell you now they don't mean a thing.
>
>   A   D
> Ev'ry place I go I think of you,
>
>   A   D
> Ev'ry song I sing I sing for you,
>
>   A   E
> When I come back I'll wear your wedding ring.

Chorus 2   *Repeat Chorus 1*

Verse 3

> A   D
> Now the time has come to leave you,
>
> A   D
> One more time let me kiss you,
>
> A   E
>   Then close your eyes, I'll be on my way.
>
> A   D
> Dream about the days to come
>
>   A   D
> When I won't have to leave ___ alone,
>
>   A   E
> A-bout the time I won't have to say…

Chorus 3

> A   D
> Kiss me and smile for me,
>
> A   D
> Tell me that you'll wait for me,
>
> A   E
> Hold me like you'll never let me go.
>
>   A   D
> I'm leaving on a jet plane,
>
> A   D
>   I don't know when I'll be back again.
>
>   A   D
> ‖: Leaving on a jet plane,
>
> A   D
>   I don't know when I'll be back again. :‖
>
> A   D   E
>   Oh, babe, I hate to go.

Just the Way You Are

Words and Music by Bruno Mars,
Ari Levine, Philip Lawrence,
Khari Cain and Khalil Walton

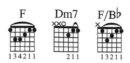

Intro
    F   Dm7   F/B♭   F
Ahh, ___ ahh, ___ ahh.

Verse 1
             F
Oh, ___ her eyes, her eyes make the stars look like they're not shinin'.

Dm7
Her hair, her hair falls perfectly without her tryin'.

F/B♭   F
She's so beautiful, and I tell her ev'ry ___ day. Yeah.

Verse 2
             F
I know, I know when I compliment her, she won't believe me.

Dm7
And it's so, it's so sad to think that she don't see what I see.

F/B♭   F
But ev'ry time she asks me, "Do I look okay?" I say:

Chorus 1
                      F   Dm7
When I see your face, ___ there's not a thing ___ that I would change,

          F/B♭   F
'Cause you're amaz - ing just the way you are.

                              Dm7
And when you smile, the whole world stops ___ and stares for a while,

          F/B♭   F
'Cause, girl, you're amaz - ing just the way you are. ___ Yeah.

Verse 3

       F

Her lips, her lips, I could kiss them all day if she'd let me.

    Dm7

Her laugh, her laugh, she hates but I think it's so sexy.

    F/B♭   F

She's so beautiful, and I tell her ev'ry ___ day.

Verse 4

       F

Oh, you know, you know, you know I'd never ask you to change.

    Dm7

If perfect's what you're searchin' for then just stay the same.

    F/B♭   F

So, ___ don't even bother askin' if you look okay. You know I'll say:

Chorus 2

                     F   Dm7

When I see your face, ___ there's not a thing ___ that I would change,

           F/B♭   F

'Cause you're amaz - ing just the way you are.

                                 Dm7

And when you smile, the whole world stops ___ and stares for a while,

           F/B♭   F

'Cause, girl, you're amaz - ing just the way you are.

                    Dm7

The way you are, the way you are.

        F/B♭   F

Girl, you're amaz - ing just the way you are.

                    Dm7

When I see your face, there's not a thing ___ that I would change,

        F/B♭   F

'Cause you're amaz - ing just the way you are.

                                 Dm7

And when you smile, the whole world stops ___ and stares for a while,

        F/B♭   F

'Cause, girl, you're amaz - ing just the way you are. ___ Yeah.

Love Me Do

Words and Music by John Lennon
and Paul McCartney

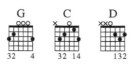

Intro

| G | C | G | C | G | C | G | | |

Chorus 1

G   C
Love, love me do.

  G   C
You know I love you.

  G   C
I'll always be true.

So please,

N.C.   G   C   G   C
Love me do. ____ Oh, love me do.

Chorus 2

Repeat Chorus 1

Bridge

D
Someone to love,

C   G
Somebody new.

D
Someone to love,

C   G
Someone like you.

Chorus 3

    G   C
Love, love me do.

        G   C
You know I love you.

      G   C
I'll always be true.

So please,

N.C.   G   C   G
Love me do. ____ Oh, love me do.

Solo

‖: D | | C |G   :‖
| | | | D |

Chorus 4

    G   C
Love, love me do.

        G   C
You know I love you.

      G   C
I'll always be true.

So please,

N.C.   G   C   G   C
Love me do. ____ Oh, love me do.

        G   C
‖: Yeah, love me do.

      G   C
Oh, love me do. :‖   *Repeat and fade*

Margaritaville

Words and Music by
Jimmy Buffett

Melody:

Nib-blin' on   sponge __ cake,

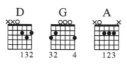

D   G   A

Intro | D | G | A | D | | |

Verse 1

        D
    Nibblin' on sponge cake, watchin' the sun bake

                             A
All of those tourists covered with oil.

Strummin' my six string on my front porch swing.

                                   D
Smell those shrimp, they're beginning to boil.

Chorus 1

G   **A**   **D**
    Wastin' a - way again in Marga - ritaville,

G   **A**   **D**
    Searchin' for my ___ lost shaker of salt.

G   **A**   **D**   **A**   **G**
    Some people claim ___ that there's a wom - an to blame,

           A   **D**
But I know ___ it's nobody's fault.

Verse 2

        D
    Don't know the reason I stayed here all season

                            A
With nothing to show but this brand-new tattoo.

But it's a real beauty, a Mexican cutie,

                    D
How it got here I haven't a clue.

Chorus 2

```
         G          A              D
         Wastin' a - way again in Marga - ritaville,

         G              A                  D
         Searchin' for my ___ lost shaker of salt.

         G                 A          D     A       G
         Some people claim ___ that there's a wom - an to blame,

                    A                    D
         Now I think, ___ hell, it could be my fault.
```

Instrumental

```
|D        |         |         |         |
|         |         |A        |         |
|G        |A        |D    A   |G        |
|A        |         |D        |         |
```

Verse 3

```
         D
         I blew out my flip-flop, stepped on a poptop,

                                         A
         Cut my heel, had to cruise on back home.

         But there's booze in the blender, and soon it will render

                                              D
         That frozen concoction that helps me hang on.
```

Chorus 3

```
         G          A              D
         Wastin' a - way again in Marga - ritaville,

         G              A                  D
         Searchin' for my ___ lost shaker of salt.

         G                  A          D     A       G
         Some people claim ___ that there's a wom - an to blame,

                    A                    D
         But I know ___ it's my own damn fault.

                 G                   A          D     A       G
         Yes, and   some people claim ___ that there's a wom - an to blame,

                    A                    D    G   A   D
         And I know ___ it's my own damn fault.
```

Me and Bobby McGee

Words and Music by Kris Kristofferson
and Fred Foster

Melody:

Bust-ed   flat ___   in Bat - on Rouge,

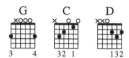

G   C   D

| | |
3   4   32 1   1 3 2

Intro |G |C |G   C |G |

Verse 1

G
Busted flat in Baton Rouge, waitin' for a train,

                                    D
When I was feelin' nearly faded as my ___ jeans.

Bobby thumbed a diesel down just before it rained;

                            G C G
They rode us all the way to New Or-leans.

Verse 2

G
I pulled my harpoon out of my dirty red bandanna,

                                    C
I was playin' soft while Bobby sang the blues, ___ yeah.

                        G
Windshield wipers slap in time, I was holdin' Bobby's hand in mine.

D
We sang ev'ry song that driver knew.

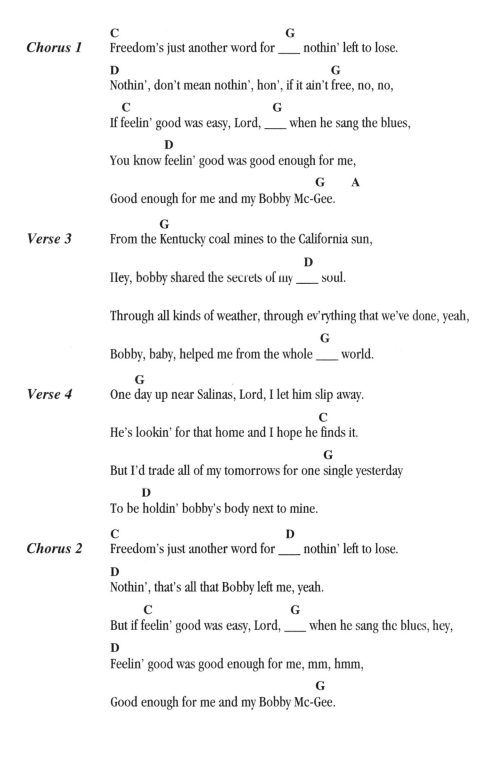

Chorus 1

    C   G
Freedom's just another word for ___ nothin' left to lose.

    D   G
Nothin', don't mean nothin', hon', if it ain't free, no, no,

     C   G
If feelin' good was easy, Lord, ___ when he sang the blues,

               D
You know feelin' good was good enough for me,

                                 G   A
Good enough for me and my Bobby Mc-Gee.

Verse 3

              G
From the Kentucky coal mines to the California sun,

                              D
Hey, bobby shared the secrets of my ___ soul.

Through all kinds of weather, through ev'rything that we've done, yeah,

                            G
Bobby, baby, helped me from the whole ___ world.

Verse 4

     G
One day up near Salinas, Lord, I let him slip away.

                            C
He's lookin' for that home and I hope he finds it.

                            G
But I'd trade all of my tomorrows for one single yesterday

          D
To be holdin' bobby's body next to mine.

Chorus 2

    C   D
Freedom's just another word for ___ nothin' left to lose.

    D
Nothin', that's all that Bobby left me, yeah.

     C   G
But if feelin' good was easy, Lord, ___ when he sang the blues, hey,

    D
Feelin' good was good enough for me, mm, hmm,

                              G
Good enough for me and my Bobby Mc-Gee.

Ring of Fire

Words and Music by Merle Kilgore
and June Carter

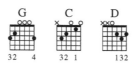

Intro

G	C	G		
	D	G		

Verse 1

    G   C   G   C G
Love is a burning thing

                    D G   D G
And it makes its fir - y ring.

                C   G C G
Bound by wild__ desires,

            D   G
I fell into a ring of fire.

Chorus 1

    D   C   G
I fell into a burning ring of fire.

        D
I went down, down, down

            C   G
And the flames went higher.

And it burns, burns, burns,

       D   G
The ring of fire,

       D   G
The ring of fire.

Interlude | G | C | G | |
                              | | D | G | |

Verse 2

                         G   C   G   C G
The taste of love is sweet

                              D   G   D G
When hearts like ours meet.

                          C   G C G
I fell for you like a child,

                        D   G
Oh, but the fire went wild.

Chorus 2   *Repeat Chorus 1*

Chorus 3   *Repeat Chorus 1*

Outro

               G
And it burns, burns, burns,

               D   G
The ring___ of fire,

               D   G
||: The ring of fire. :|| *Repeat and fade*

Seven Bridges Road

Words and Music by
Stephen T. Young

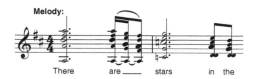

There   are ____ stars   in the

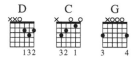

Verse 1

N.C.
There are stars in the southern sky,

Southward as you go.

There is moonlight and moss in the trees

Down the Seven Bridges Road.

Interlude

D			C		
G	D				

Verse 2

     D   **C**   **G**   **D**
Now I have loved you like a ba - by,

         C   **G** **D**
Like some lonesome child.

         C   **G**   **D**
And I have loved you in a tame ___ way,

         C **G** **D**
And I have loved wild.

Bridge

         C   **D**
Some-times there's a part ___ of me

         C   **D**
Has to turn from here and go.

C   **D**
Runnin' like a child from these warm stars

          C   **G** **D**
Down the Seven Bridges Road.

Verse 3

N.C.
There are stars in the southern sky,

And if ever you decide you should go,

There is a taste of time sweet and honey

Down the Seven Bridges Road.

Shelter from the Storm

Words and Music by
Bob Dylan

Melody:

'Twas in an-oth-er life-time,

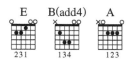

E   B(add4)   A

231   134   123

Intro ‖: E | | | :‖

Verse 1
E   Badd4   A   E
'Twas in another life - time,   one of toil and blood,

                Badd4   A
When blackness was a vir - tue and the road ___ was full of mud.

E   Badd4   A
I came in from the wild - erness, a creature void of form.

        E   Badd4
"Come in," she said, "I'll give ___ ya

A   E   Badd4   A   E   Badd4   A   E
Shelter from the storm."

Verse 2
        E   Badd4   A   E
And if I pass this way ___ again, you can rest assured

                Badd4   A
I'll always do my best ___ for her, on that I give my word,

            E   Badd4   A
In a world ___ of steel-eyed death, and men who are fighting to be warm.

        E   Badd4
"Come in," she said, "I'll give ___ ya

A   E   Badd4   A   E
Shelter from the storm."

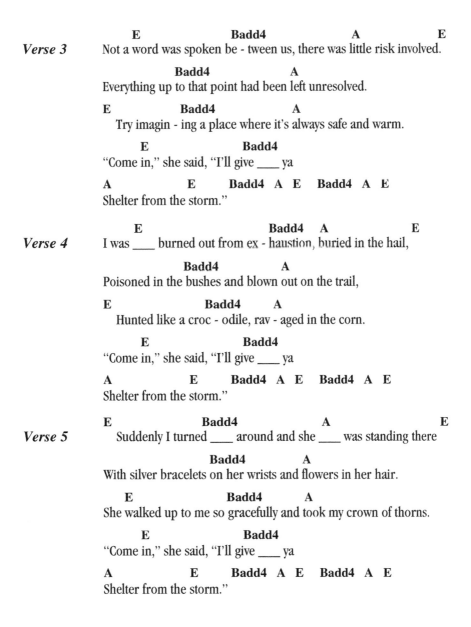

Verse 3
```
        E                Badd4              A           E
Not a word was spoken be - tween us, there was little risk involved.

            Badd4            A
Everything up to that point had been left unresolved.

E            Badd4            A
   Try imagin - ing a place where it's always safe and warm.

        E                Badd4
"Come in," she said, "I'll give ____ ya

A            E        Badd4  A  E    Badd4  A  E
Shelter from the storm."
```

Verse 4
```
        E                    Badd4    A            E
I was ____ burned out from ex - haustion, buried in the hail,

            Badd4            A
Poisoned in the bushes and blown out on the trail,

E            Badd4        A
   Hunted like a croc - odile, rav - aged in the corn.

        E                Badd4
"Come in," she said, "I'll give ____ ya

A            E        Badd4  A  E    Badd4  A  E
Shelter from the storm."
```

Verse 5
```
E            Badd4                A              E
   Suddenly I turned ____ around and she ____ was standing there

            Badd4            A
With silver bracelets on her wrists and flowers in her hair.

    E                Badd4        A
She walked up to me so gracefully and took my crown of thorns.

        E                Badd4
"Come in," she said, "I'll give ____ ya

A            E        Badd4  A  E    Badd4  A  E
Shelter from the storm."
```

Verse 6

E   Badd4   A   E
Now there is a wall be - tween us, somethin' there's been lost.

                      Badd4   A
I took too much for grant - ed, I got ___ my signals crossed.

E   Badd4   A
Just to think that it all ___ began on a non-eventful morn.

         E   Badd4
"Come in," she said, "I'll give ___ ya

A   E   Badd4 A E   Badd4 A E
Shelter from the storm."

Verse 7

          E   Badd4   A   E
Well, the deputy walks on hard nails and the preacher rides a mount,

                Badd4   A
But nothing really mat - ters much, it's doom alone that counts.

       E   Badd4   A
And the one eyed under - taker, he blows a futile horn.

       E   Badd4
"Come in," she said, "I'll give ___ ya

A   E   Badd4 A E   Badd4 A E
Shelter from the storm."

Verse 8

E   Badd4   A   E
I've heard newborn ba - bies wailin' like a mournin' dove

                Badd4   A
And old men with broken teeth strand - ed without love.

       E   Badd4   A
Do I understand your ques - tion, man? Is it hopeless and forlorn?

       E   Badd4
"Come in," she said, "I'll give ___ ya

A   E   Badd4 A E   Badd4 A E
Shelter from the storm."

Verse 9

```
        E              Badd4          A                   E
In a little hill top vil - lage, they gam - bled for my clothes.

                      Badd4          A
I bargained for salva - tion and she give me a lethal dose.

    E              Badd4      A
I offered up my innocence I got repaid with scorn.

        E                  Badd4
"Come in," she said, "I'll give ____ ya

A                 E       Badd4  A  E   Badd4  A  E
Shelter from the storm."
```

Verse 10

```
            E                  Badd4          A                   E
Well, I'm livin' in a foreign coun - try but I'm bound to cross the line.

            Badd4                A
Beauty walks a ra - zor's edge, some-day I'll make it mine.

        E            Badd4                A
If I could only turn back ____ the clock to when God and her were born.

        E                  Badd4
"Come in," she said, "I'll give ____ ya

A                 E       Badd4  A  E  Badd4  A
Shelter from the storm."
```

Outro

```
‖: E      | Badd4   | A        |              :‖  Play 6 times
 | E      | Badd4   | A        | E            |
```

Squeeze Box

Words and Music by
Peter Townshend

Melody:

Ma - ma's got a squeeze-box

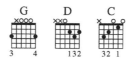

G   D   C

Intro

‖: G   D | G   D   :‖

‖: G | :‖

Verse 1

        G
Ma - ma's got a squeeze box

She wears on her chest.

From when Daddy comes home,

He never gets no rest.

        D
Because she's playin' all night.

     C
And the music's alright.

     D
Ma - ma's got a squeeze box,

     C
Dad - dy never sleeps at night.

‖: G | :‖

	G
Verse 2	Well, the kids don't eat

G

Verse 2   Well, the kids don't eat

C

And the dog can't sleep.

There's no escape from the music

In the whole damn street.

D

Because she's playin' all night.

C

And the music's alright.

D

Ma - ma's got a squeeze box,

C

Dad - dy never sleeps at night.

‖: **G**   :‖

G

Chorus 1   She goes in and out, and in and out,

And in and out, and in and out.

D

She's playin' all night,

C

And the music's alright.

D

Ma - ma's got a squeeze box,

C

Dad - dy never sleeps at night.

‖: **G**   :‖

	G **C G**
Bridge	She goes squeeze me. Come on and squeeze me.

                                                      G   **C G**

Bridge

She goes squeeze me. Come on and squeeze me.

               D

Come on and tease me like you do,

    C

I'm so in love with you.

      D

Ma - ma's got a squeeze box,

     C   **G**

Dad - dy never sleeps at night.

Banjo Solo

```
‖: G        |        :‖
 | D        |        |
 | C        |        |
 | D        | C      |
 | G        |        |
```

Chorus 2

       G

She goes in and out, and in and out,

And in and out and in and out.

     D

She's playin' all night,

      C

And the music's alright.

     D

Ma - ma's got a squeeze box,

     C   **G C**   **G**

Dad - dy never sleeps at night.   Wah - oo.

This Land Is Your Land

Words and Music by
Woody Guthrie

(Capo 3rd fret)

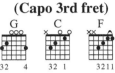

Intro | G | | C | | | |

                    F   **C**

Chorus 1   This land is your land and this land is my land

                  G   **C**

From Cali-fornia to the New York island.

                            F   **C**

From the redwood forest to the Gulf Stream waters,

G   **C**

This land was made for you and me.

                  F   **C**

Verse 1   As I was walking that ribbon of highway,

                G   **C**

I saw a-bove me that endless skyway,

                F   **C**

I saw be-low me that golden valley.

G   **C**

This land was made for you and me.

Interlude	|F	|	|C	|	|
	|	|G	|C	|	|

Verse 2

              F   **C**
I've roamed and rambled and I followed my footsteps

              G   **C**
To the sparkling sands of her diamond deserts.

   F   **C**
All a-round me, a voice was sounding,

G   **C**
This land was made for you and me.

Verse 3

              F   **C**
When the sun came shining, and I was strolling,

              G   **C**
And the wheat fields waving, and the dust clouds rolling,

          F   **C**
As the fog was lifting a voice was chanting:

 G   **C**
"This land was made for you and me."

Chorus 2   **Repeat Chorus 1**

Verse 4

          F   **C**
As I went walking, I saw a sign there,

           G   **C**
And on the sign it said "No Tres-passing."

           F   **C**
But on the other side it didn't say nothing.

G   **C**
This side was made for you and me.

Verse 5
                                         F   C

```
                          F              C
Verse 5    In the shadow of the steeple I saw my people,

                   G              C
           By the re-lief office I seen my people;

                          F              C
           As they stood there hungry, I stood there asking:

           G                      C
           Is this land made for you and me?


                   F          C
Verse 6    Nobody living can ever stop me,

                   G              C
           As I go walking that freedom highway;

                   F                      C
           Nobody living can ever make me turn back.

           G                      C
           This land was made for you and me.
```

Chorus 3   **Repeat Chorus 1**

Outro
```
| F    | C    |      |      |      |
| G    | C    |      |      |      |
| F    | C    |      |      |      |
| G    | C    |      |      |      |
```

Sunshine Superman

Words and Music by
Donovan Leitch

Melody:

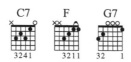

Sun - shine _ came soft - ly through my

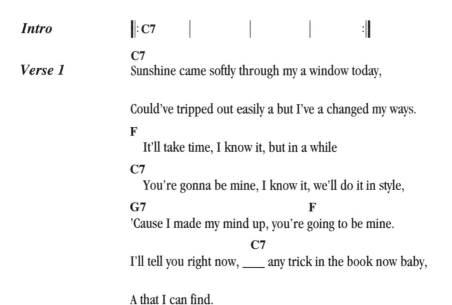

C7   F   G7
3241   3211 32   1

Intro   ‖: C7 | | | :‖

Verse 1
C7
Sunshine came softly through my a window today,

Could've tripped out easily a but I've a changed my ways.

F
It'll take time, I know it, but in a while

C7
You're gonna be mine, I know it, we'll do it in style,

G7   **F**
'Cause I made my mind up, you're going to be mine.

                         C7
I'll tell you right now, ____ any trick in the book now baby,

A that I can find.

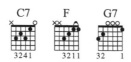

Verse 2

C7
Ev'rybody's hustlin' just to have a little scene.

When I say we'll be cool I think that you know what I mean.

F
We stood on the beach at sunset, do you remember when?

C7
I know a beach where baby, a it never ends.

G7   F
When you've made your mind up, for-ever to be mine.

C7
I'll pick up your hand and slowly, blow your little mind.

G7   F
'Cause I made my mind up, you're going to be mine.

                              C7
I'll tell you right now, ____ any trick in the book, now, baby,

A that I can find.

Interlude

| C7 | | | | |

Verse 3

C7
Superman or Green Lantern ain't got a nothin' on me,

I can make like a turtle and dive for pearls in the sea.

F
A you, you, you can just sit there a thinkin' on your velvet throne

C7
'Bout all the rainbows a you can a have for your own,

G7   F
When you've made your mind up for-ever to be mine.

Outro

    C7
‖: I'll pick up your hand and slowly blow your little mind,

G7
When you've made your mind up

    F
For-ever to be mine. :‖ *Repeat and fade*

Time for Me to Fly

Words and Music by
Kevin Cronin

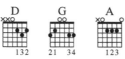

Intro ‖: D   G |A   G   :‖

Verse 1

D
I've been around for you,

    A
I've been up and down for you,

    G   D
But I__ just can't get any relief.

I've swallowed my pride for you,

A
    Lived and lied for you,

    G   D
But a you still make me feel like a thief.

             A
You got me stealin' your love away

    G   D
'Cause a you never give it.

A
Peelin' the years away

    G   D
And a we can't re-live it.

  G   D
Oh, I make you laugh,

    G   D
And a you make me cry.

A
    I believe it's time for me to fly.

‖: **D**   **G**   │**A**   **G**   :‖

Verse 2

D
You said we'd work it out,

   A
You said that you had no doubt,

   G   **D**
That deep down we were really in love.

D
Oh, but I'm tired of holdin' on

   A
To feelin' I know is gone.

G   **D**
   I do believe that I've had enough.

   D **A**
I've had e-nough of the falseness

      G   **D**
Of a worn - out re-lation.

   A
E-nough of the jealousy

      G   **D**
And the intolera - tion.

   G   **D**
Oh, I make you laugh,

     G   **D**
And a you make me cry.

A   **D**   **N.C.**
   I believe it's time for me to fly.

Chorus 1

               A   **G**   **D**
(Time for me to fly.)

                Oh, I've got to set__ myself free.

               A   **G**   **D**
(Time for me to fly.)

                Ah, that's just how it's a got to   be.

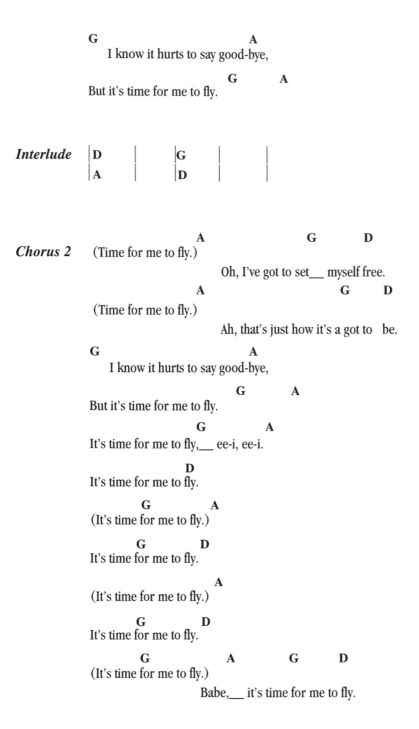

G   A
I know it hurts to say good-bye,

                        G   A
But it's time for me to fly.

Interlude | D | | G | | |
              | A | | D | | |

                             A   G   D
Chorus 2   (Time for me to fly.)

                                       Oh, I've got to set__ myself free.

                           A   G   D
(Time for me to fly.)

                               Ah, that's just how it's a got to   be.

G   A
I know it hurts to say good-bye,

                        G   A
But it's time for me to fly.

                 G   A
It's time for me to fly,__ ee-i, ee-i.

                D
It's time for me to fly.

         G   A
(It's time for me to fly.)

         G   D
It's time for me to fly.

               A
(It's time for me to fly.)

         G   D
It's time for me to fly.

         G   A   G   D
(It's time for me to fly.)

                         Babe,__ it's time for me to fly.

What I Got

Words and Music by Brad Nowell,
Eric Wilson, Floyd Gaugh and
Lindon Roberts

Ear - ly   in   the morn - in',

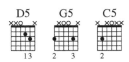

Intro

| D5   G5 | D5   G5 |

Verse 1

    D5   G5 D5   G5
Early in the morn - in', risin' to the street.

    D5   G5
Light me up that cigarette and I

    D5   G5
Strap shoes on my feet. (De, de, de, de, de.)

    D5   G5 D5   G5
Got to find a rea - son, reason things went wrong.

    D5   G5   D5   G5
Got to find a reason why my money's all gone.

      D5   G5   D5   G5
I ___ got a Dalma - tion and I can still get high.

      D5   G5   D5   G5
I ___ can play the guitar like a motherfuckin' riot.

Interlude 1

‖: D5   G5 | D5   G5 :‖

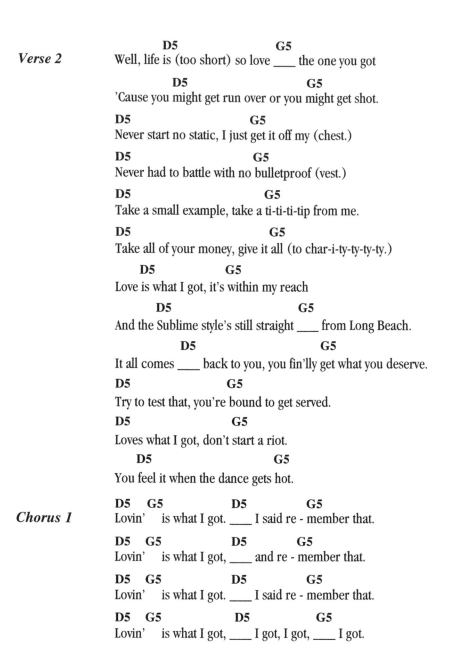

Verse 2
       D5   **G5**
Well, life is (too short) so love ____ the one you got

        D5   **G5**
'Cause you might get run over or you might get shot.

D5   **G5**
Never start no static, I just get it off my (chest.)

D5   **G5**
Never had to battle with no bulletproof (vest.)

D5   **G5**
Take a small example, take a ti-ti-ti-tip from me.

D5   **G5**
Take all of your money, give it all (to char-i-ty-ty-ty-ty.)

   D5   **G5**
Love is what I got, it's within my reach

      D5   **G5**
And the Sublime style's still straight ____ from Long Beach.

          D5   **G5**
It all comes ____ back to you, you fin'lly get what you deserve.

D5   **G5**
Try to test that, you're bound to get served.

D5   **G5**
Loves what I got, don't start a riot.

   D5   **G5**
You feel it when the dance gets hot.

Chorus 1
D5 **G5**   **D5**   **G5**
Lovin'   is what I got. ____ I said re - member that.

D5 **G5**   **D5**   **G5**
Lovin'   is what I got, ____ and re - member that.

D5 **G5**   **D5**   **G5**
Lovin'   is what I got. ____ I said re - member that.

D5 **G5**   **D5**   **G5**
Lovin'   is what I got, ____ I got, I got, ____ I got.

Verse 3

D5   G5
Why, I don't cry when my dog runs away.

D5   G5
I don't get angry at the bills I have to pay.

D5   G5
I don't get angry when my mom smokes pot,

D5   G5
Hits the bottle and moves right to the rock.

D5   G5
Fuckin' and fightin', it's all the same.

 D5   G5
Livin' with Louie Dog's the only way to stay sane.

D5   G5   D5
 Let the lovin', let the lovin' come back ___ to me.

Interlude 2 ‖: D5 C5 G5 |D5 C5 G5 :‖ D5 | |

Chorus 2

   D5 C5 G5   D5   C5   G5
'Cause lovin' is what I got. ___ I said re - member that.

  D5 C5 G5   D5   C5   G5
Lov - in' is what I got, ___ and re - member that.

  D5 C5 G5   D5   C5   G5
Lov - in' is what I got. ___ I said re - member that.

  D5 C5 G5   D5   C5   G5
Lov - in' is what I got, ___ I got, I got, ___ I got.

Outro |D5 G5 |D5 G5 |D5 ‖

Used to Love Her

Words and Music by W. Axl Rose, Slash,
Izzy Stradlin', Duff McKagan and Steven Adler

Melody:

I used to love __ her,

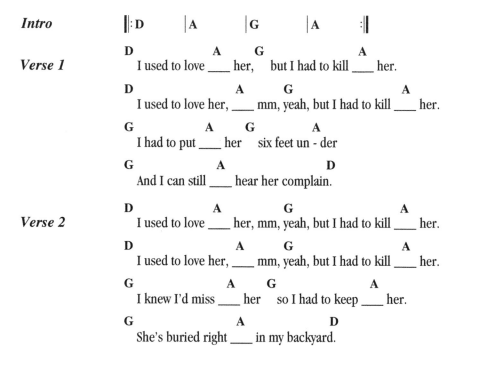

D   A   G

D xx0   A x0   G 00

1 3 2   1 2 3   2 1   3 4

Intro   ‖: D |A |G |A   :‖

Verse 1

D   A   G   A
I used to love ___ her,   but I had to kill ___ her.

D   A   G   A
I used to love her, ___ mm, yeah, but I had to kill ___ her.

G   A   G   A
I had to put ___ her   six feet un - der

G   A   D
And I can still ___ hear her complain.

Verse 2

D   A   G   A
I used to love ___ her, mm, yeah, but I had to kill ___ her.

D   A   G   A
I used to love her, ___ mm, yeah, but I had to kill ___ her.

G   A   G   A
I knew I'd miss ___ her   so I had to keep ___ her.

G   A   D
She's buried right ___ in my backyard.

Guitar Solo 1   *Repeat Verse 1 (Instrumental)*

Verse 3

D   A   G   A
I used to love ___ her,   but I had to kill ___ her.

D   A   G   A
I used to love her, ___ mm, yeah, but I had to kill ___ her.

G   A   G   A
She bitched so much   she drove me nuts.

G   A   D
And now we're hap - pier this way.

Guitar Solo 2   *Repeat Verse 1 (Instrumental)*

Verse 4

D   A   G   A
I used to love ___ her,   but I had to kill ___ her.

D   A   G   A
I used to love her, ___ mm, yeah, but I had to kill ___ her.

G   A   G   A
I had to put ___ her, oo, ___ six feet un - der

G   A   D
And I can still ___ hear her complain.

You Are My Sunshine

Words and Music by
Jimmie Davis

Melody:

The oth - er night dear... _____

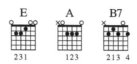

E   A   B7

231   123   213 4

Verse 1

         E
The other night dear as I lay sleeping,

       A   **E**
I dreamed I held you in my arms.

       A   **E**
When I a-woke dear I was mis-taken,

      B7   **E**
And I hung my head and cried:

Chorus 1

         E
You are my sunshine, my only sunshine,

       A   **E**
You make me happy when skies are gray.

       A   **E**
You'll never know dear how much I love you.

      B7   **E**
Please don't take my sunshine a-way.

Verse 2

                           E
I'll always love you and make you happy,

           A   **E**
If you will only say the same.

          A   **E**
But if you leave me to love an-other

            B7   **E**
You'll regret it all some day.

Chorus 2   ***Repeat Chorus 1***

Verse 3

                   E
You told me once dear you really loved me,

          A   **E**
And no one else could come be-tween.

            A   **E**
But now you've left me and love an-other;

           B7   **E**
You have shattered all my dreams.

Chorus 3   ***Repeat Chorus 1***

You Don't Mess Around with Jim

Words and Music by
Jim Croce

Melody:

Up - town got its hust - lers,

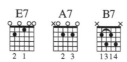

E7   A7   B7

2 1	2 3	1 3 1 4

Intro | **E7** | | | | | | | |

Verse 1

E7
Uptown got its hustlers, the bow'ry got its bums.

Forty-second street got big Jim a Walker.

He a pool shootin' son of a gun.

      A7
Yeah, he big ___ and dumb as a man can come,

But he's stronger than a country horse.

      B7   **A7**
And when the bad folks all get to - gether at night

      B7   **A7**   **E7**
You know they all call big Jim, "Boss," ___ just because.

And they say,

	A7 **E7**
Chorus 1	"You don't tug on Superman's cape,

Chorus 1

    A7   **E7**
"You don't tug on Superman's cape,

    A7   **E7**
You don't spit into the wind,

    A7
You don't pull the mask off that old Lone Ranger,

    B7   **E7**
And you don't mess around with Jim."

                    B7
A, doo, 'n, doo, da, da, dce, dee, 'n, dee, dee, dee.

Verse 2

    E7
Well, out of south Alabama come a country boy.

He said, "I'm lookin' for a man named Jim.

I am a pool shootin' boy. My name is Willie McCoy,

But down a home they call me, 'Slim.

    A7
Yeah, I'm look - in' for the king of Forty-second Street.

He drivin' a drop top Cadillac.

      B7   **A7**
Last week he took ___ all my money in it may sound funny,

  B7   **A7**
But I come to get my money back."

    E7
And ev'rybody say, "Jack, woo, don't you know that…

Chorus 2   *Repeat Chorus 1*

		E7
Verse 3		Well, a hush fell over the pool room

Verse 3

E7
Well, a hush fell over the pool room

'Till Jim, he come boppin' in off the street.

And when the cuttin' was done the only part that wasn't bloody

Was the soles of the big man's feet. Woo.
      A7
Yeah, he was cut in 'bout a hundred places,

And he was shot in a couple more.
      B7   **A7**
And you better believe I sung a diff'rent kind of story
      B7   **A7**   **E7**
When, a, big Jim hit the floor. ___ Oh.

Yeah, they sing…

Chorus 3

      A7   **E7**
"You don't tug on Superman's cape,

      A7   **E7**
You don't spit into the wind,

      A7
You don't pull the mask off that old Lone Ranger,

      B7   **E7**
And you don't mess around with Slim." ___ Hmm.

Breakdown

E7
   Yeah, Big Jim got his hat. Find out where it's at.

It's not hustlin' people strange to you.

Even if you do got a two-piece, custom-made pool cue. Hm, hm.

Chorus 4   *Repeat Chorus 3*

Outro   ‖: E7 | :‖ *Repeat and fade w/ vocal ad lib.*

Guitar Chord Songbooks

Each book includes complete lyrics, chord symbols, and guitar chord diagrams.

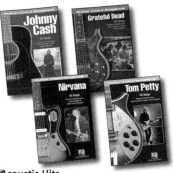

Acoustic Hits
00701787 . . . . $14.99

Acoustic Rock
00699540 . . . . $19.99

Alabama
00699914 . . . . $14.95

The Beach Boys
00699566 . . . . $15.99

The Beatles (A-I)
00699558 . . . . $17.99

The Beatles (J-Y)
00699562 . . . . $17.99

Bluegrass
00702585 . . . . $14.99

Johnny Cash
00699648 . . . . $17.99

Steven Curtis Chapman
00700702 . . . . $17.99

Children's Songs
00699539 . . . . $16.99

Christmas Carols
00699536 . . . . $12.99

Christmas Songs – 2nd Ed.
00119911 . . . . $14.99

Eric Clapton
00699567 . . . . $16.99

Classic Rock
00699598 . . . . $15.99

Coffeehouse Hits
00703318 . . . . $14.99

Country
00699534 . . . . $14.95

Country Favorites
00700609 . . . . $14.99

Country Hits
00140859 . . . . $14.99

Country Standards
00700608 . . . . $12.95

Cowboy Songs
00699636 . . . . $14.99

Creedence Clearwater Revival
00701786 . . . . $14.99

Jim Croce
00148087 . . . . $14.99

Crosby, Stills & Nash
00701609 . . . . $12.99

John Denver
02501697 . . . . $14.99

Neil Diamond
00700606 . . . . $15.99

Disney
00701071 . . . . $16.99

Best of Bob Dylan
14037617 . . . . $17.99

Eagles
00122917 . . . . $16.99

Early Rock
00699916 . . . . $14.99

Folk Pop Rock
00699651 . . . . $15.99

Folksongs
00699541 . . . . $14.99

40 Easy Strumming Songs
00115972 . . . . $14.99

Four Chord Songs
00701611 . . . . $12.99

Glee
00702501 . . . . $14.99

Gospel Hymns
00700463 . . . . $14.99

Grand Ole Opry®
00699885 . . . . $16.95

Grateful Dead
00139461 . . . . $14.99

Green Day
00103074 . . . . $12.99

Guitar Chord Songbook White Pages
00702609 . . . . $29.99

Irish Songs
00701044 . . . . $14.99

Michael Jackson
00137847 . . . . $14.99

Billy Joel
00699632 . . . . $16.99

Elton John
00699732 . . . . $15.99

Ray LaMontagne
00130337 . . . . $12.99

Latin Songs
00700973 . . . . $14.99

Love Songs
00701043 . . . . $14.99

Bob Marley
00701704 . . . . $12.99

Bruno Mars
00125332 . . . . $12.99

Visit Hal Leonard online at
www.halleonard.com

Prices, contents, and availability
subject to change without notice.

Paul McCartney
00385035 . . . . $16.95

Steve Miller
00701146 . . . . $12.99

Modern Worship
00701801 . . . . $16.99

Motown
00699734 . . . . $16.95

Willie Nelson
00148273 . . . . $14.99

Nirvana
00699762 . . . . $16.99

Rock Ballads
00701034 . . . . $14.99

Roy Orbison
00699752 . . . . $14.99

Peter, Paul & Mary
00103013 . . . . $14.99

Tom Petty
00699883 . . . . $15.99

Pink Floyd
00139116 . . . . $14.99

Pop/Rock
00699538 . . . . $14.95

Praise & Worship
00699634 . . . . $14.99

Elvis Presley
00699633 . . . . $14.95

Queen
00702395 . . . . $12.99

Red Hot Chili Peppers
00699710 . . . . $17.99

Rock Ballads
00701034 . . . . $14.99

The Rolling Stones
00137716 . . . . $14.99

Bob Seger
00701147 . . . . $12.99

Carly Simon
00121011 . . . . $14.99

Sting
00699921 . . . . $14.99

Taylor Swift – 2nd Ed.
00263755 . . . . $16.99

Three Chord Acoustic Songs
00123860 . . . . $14.99

Three Chord Songs
00699720 . . . . $14.99

Two-Chord Songs
00119236 . . . . $14.99

U2
00137744 . . . . $14.99

Hank Williams
00700607 . . . . $14.99

Stevie Wonder
00120862 . . . . $14.99

Neil Young – Decade
00700464 . . . . $14.99

00699569	**2. ACOUSTIC** $16.99	00701356	**119. AC/DC CLASSICS** $17.99
00699573	**3. HARD ROCK** $17.99	00701508	**121. U2** $16.99
00699575	**7. BLUES** $17.99	00701687	**125. JEFF BECK** $16.99
00699582	**14. BLUES ROCK** $16.99	00701701	**126. BOB MARLEY** $16.99
00699584	**16. JAZZ** $15.95	00701906	**134. AVENGED SEVENFOLD** $16.99
00699580	**20. ROCKABILLY** $16.99	00702370	**139. GARY MOORE** $16.99
00699635	**23. SURF** $15.99	00702396	**140. MORE STEVIE RAY VAUGHAN** $17.99
00699649	**24. ERIC CLAPTON** $17.99	00702425	**143. SLASH** $19.99
00699643	**26. ELVIS PRESLEY** $16.99	00702532	**145. DEF LEPPARD** $17.99
00699656	**33. ACOUSTIC CLASSICS** $17.99	00702533	**146. ROBERT JOHNSON** $16.99
00699663	**38. BLUES** $16.95	14041591	**147. SIMON & GARFUNKEL** $16.99
00211597	**42. COVER BAND HITS** $16.99	14041592	**148. BOB DYLAN** $16.99
00699681	**43. LYNYRD SKYNYRD** $17.95	14041503	**149. AC/DC HITS** $17.99
00699723	**47. JIMI HENDRIX EXPERIENCE – SMASH HITS** $19.99	02501751	**152. JOE BONAMASSA** $19.99
00699724	**48. AEROSMITH CLASSICS** $17.99	00702990	**153. RED HOT CHILI PEPPERS** $19.99
00699725	**49. STEVIE RAY VAUGHAN** $17.99	00703085	**155. ERIC CLAPTON – FROM THE ALBUM UNPLUGGED** $16.99
00110269	**50. VAN HALEN 1978-1984** $17.99	00703770	**156. SLAYER** $17.99
00699728	**52. FUNK** $15.99	00101382	**157. FLEETWOOD MAC** $16.99
00702347	**59. CHET ATKINS** $16.99	00102593	**159. WES MONTGOMERY** $19.99
00699802	**63. CREEDENCE CLEARWATER REVIVAL** $16.99	00102641	**160. T-BONE WALKER** $16.99
00699803	**64. OZZY OSBOURNE** $17.99	00102659	**161. THE EAGLES – ACOUSTIC** $17.99
00699807	**66. ROLLING STONES** $17.99	00102667	**162. EAGLES HITS** $17.99
00699808	**67. BLACK SABBATH** $16.99	00210343	**165. GREEN DAY** $17.99
00699809	**68. PINK FLOYD – DARK SIDE OF THE MOON** $16.99	00111938	**167. DREAM THEATER** $24.99
00699882	**75. TOM PETTY** $16.99	00119670	**172. THE DOOBIE BROTHERS** $16.99
00699910	**77. BLUEGRASS** $15.99	00119907	**173. TRANS-SIBERIAN ORCHESTRA** $19.99
00700132	**78. NIRVANA** $16.99	00122119	**174. SCORPIONS** $16.99
00700133	**79. NEIL YOUNG** $24.99	00122127	**175. MICHAEL SCHENKER** $16.99
00700269	**85. THE POLICE** $16.99	00122132	**176. BLUES BREAKERS WITH JOHN MAYALL & ERIC CLAPTON** $19.99
00700465	**86. BOSTON** $16.99		
00700505	**91. BLUES INSTRUMENTALS** $15.99	00123271	**177. ALBERT KING** $16.99
00700506	**92. EARLY ROCK INSTRUMENTALS** $15.99	00138161	**182. SOUNDGARDEN** $17.99
00700508	**94. SLOW BLUES** $16.99	00138258	**184. KENNY WAYNE SHEPHERD** $17.99
00700509	**95. BLUES CLASSICS** $15.99	00139457	**185. JOE SATRIANI** $17.99
00211615	**96. BEST COUNTRY HITS** $16.99	00139459	**186. GRATEFUL DEAD** $17.99
00236542	**97. CHRISTMAS CLASSICS** $14.99	00140839	**187. JOHN DENVER** $17.99
00700762	**99. ZZ TOP** $16.99	00144350	**189. JOHN MAYER** $17.99
00700466	**100. B.B. KING** $16.99	00146164	**191. PINK FLOYD CLASSICS** $17.99
00701917	**101. SONGS FOR BEGINNERS** $14.99	00151352	**192. JUDAS PRIEST** $17.99
00700846	**104. DUANE ALLMAN** $16.99	00234291	**195. METALLICA: 1983-1988** $19.99
00701069	**107. CREAM** $16.99		
00701055	**110. SLIDE GUITAR HITS** $16.99		
00701052	**112. QUEEN** $16.99		
00701058	**113. JIM CROCE** $16.99		
00701060	**114. BON JOVI** $16.99		
00701070	**115. JOHNNY CASH** $16.99		
00701124	**116. THE VENTURES** $16.99		
00701224	**117. BRAD PAISLEY** $16.99		
00701353	**118. ERIC JOHNSON** $16.99		

Check out these series highlights. Complete series list and song lists available online.

Prices, contents, and availability subject to change without notice.

HAL•LEONARD®

www.halleonard.com

0311
05